Rand Amandaness

Amanda Fensome

/ BookLeaf
Publishing

India | USA | UK

Presentation by *BookLeaf Publishing*

Web: www.bookleafpub.com

E-mail: info@bookleafpub.com

ISBN: 9789358314991

First edition 2023

*For my mum, who is gone but not forgotten,
and my dad, the loveable knucklehead because
it is in the jeans.*

ACKNOWLEDGEMENT

Let's go through who to thank step by step. I would like to express my appreciation for:

Charly Lester and the Rebel Badge Club, for the badge related motivation to finally complete a writing project (it's only taken almost 30 years for me to follow through on the dream).

My housemate Tim for his general support and chipping in some funds towards me being able to take on this spontaneous challenge.

Bookleaf Publishing, for the Facebook ad for the Write Angle Challenge which gave me the last shove needed to actually get something published (and the support with the publishing process of course).

Tamlin for supporting me with random comments and likes on poetry related WhatsApp messages that I sent at all times of day.

My dad and all my other friends and family who have helped make me, me and have provided inspiration of the years. Keep being yourselves, everyone.

PREFACE

The journey to this anthology has been both quick and slow. I have written poetry on and off since I was about 13 and I hit my stereotypical teenage angst stage. I have considered publishing my work multiple times over the years but never felt I had the material needed to do so. Then along came Rebel Badge Club.

I won't bore you with the detail here. It is enough to say that the club challenges you try new things and revisit old ones and in doing so you get badges. One of the badges is Writer. There are multiple ways to complete it and I had intended to tackle it by writing a review blog of books, films and so on. Except it turns out I am not very good at being consistent in that.

One day, I was scrolling through Facebook and there was an advert for the Write Angle Challenge from Bookleaf Publishing. I was curious and looked it up. All of a sudden, here was my way of completing the badge. Here was the way to finally get around to publishing some of my writing. I signed right up.

Then it hit me what a challenge I had set myself. I looked back over some previous poems and found I only had 3 or 4 that I thought I could use if I polished them up. I had few ideas of where to start writing another 20+ plus poems so I could choose the best ones. There were a few days of panic and a whole week where I barely wrote at all!

Luckily, I tend to work best when a deadline is almost on top of me. With 5 days to go I went from 10 poems to 24. All that time where I hadn't been writing my brain had been working, creating and all I needed to do was let it all out in a brainstorming mess. I had enough ideas from that creative vomit for multiple anthologies, the key was finding threads and themes that connected them together.

Me being me though, not all the ideas would fit a theme. Eventually I realised how perfect those things that didn't really fit were. They are some of the random elements and stories and moments that make me who I am. I spontaneously made the decision to publish an anthology in the first place so shouldn't that book be as equally varied and eclectic? Shouldn't this book reflect me?

I am sorry (not sorry) to welcome you to this distillation of random Amandaness.

21 days, 21 Lines

Pain shoots down, knee buckles and then it's
gone. Damn back!
Encountering my teenage self makes me feel sad
for her. My heart aches.
First lesson with my refugee student in 2
months: he has improved so much!
Rebel Fun: Geocaching, still life, improv,
collage and Bollywood dance.
Sunday, rest day? Nah! Re-arranging furniture,
organising stuff, roast dinner, awesome rugby!
Tired now. Lots of 'colouring' to complete my
hummingbird artwork.
Just another day of frustrating students. Why
does she squeak at me?
Descriptive writing and sessions full of pep.
Back is definitely better!
Prison stories and debates on who might be able
to beat Bronson in a fight. Teens are weird.
Weighed myself. Wished I hadn't. I am F-A-T!!!
Rugby is obviously my spectator sport. England
lost their semi-final by a point, and I am gutted!
Chill day of hot tub, tea and cakes, and King of
Tokyo.
A lie in and a nap, plenty of cat hugs, chicken
nuggets and listening to Poe.

Feather art is done! (for now) Fish finger sandwiches and Life on Mars.

Enjoying my rest week. I could get lots done but my body has gone 'NOPE'.

Oh, what a lie-in! 10am. Feeling refreshed. It's a shame about the headache.

Poetry day – inspiration has finally struck.

Lucky, since there are only 4 more writing days.

I do love a Call of Cthulhu game, just bad luck it isn't Halloween. Or maybe, that's good luck?

A post-mortem live? So very interesting. Good job I am ok with a little gore.

The break is over, back to the teenagers. I will get them to learn something!

This is Halloween, Halloween, Halloween…

Sadly, I'm old so didn't do much.

My Life in Thirty-Three Words

Premature, breathing?
Crying; MEN!
Penguins, Erica, Cornwall.
Death, home.
'Piggy', chess, Adam.
Ashcroft, 'Leech',
Vampires, blood, emo, art.
Degree, Arabic, Hesh, Depression.
Prison, awakening, DEATH!
Galapagos.
Grief, debt, vocation?
Lockdowns, housemate, cats.
Growing.

The Early History of Me

Decided I should be free, so, I arrived 2 months
early.
December the fifth 1989 - I obviously wanted
Christmas!
Jet-black hair and jet-black eyes (Wish I could
have kept those).
So tiny, all my clothes were huge.

New Year's Eve, I start the curse and stop
breathing a few times.
I even turned blue. It drove my parents crazy.
The doctors and nurses didn't believe them. So, I
did it again!
I was such a little cow-bag.

Used to cry all evening if it was Dad's bowling
night.
Scream and bawl from the moment he closed the
door until he came home.
Even if he went on a different night, I would
wind up Mum with my noise.
What a lady dog I was!

The presence of all men, except my dad, used to
make me cry.

Mum couldn't take me anywhere! New doctors,
new dentist...
Took ages for anyone to work out the problem
and fix it.
The cure? Throwing knitted clowns.

Teenagers Suck

All teenagers suck!
Mean, moody, bags of hormones.
You fit… or you don't.

Outsider

I'm forever on the outside,
Always looking in.
The last to know,
The first one ignored.
I'm there… but not there.
Included only on the fringes.
The watcher.
An isolated observer.
Trying to understand the rules.
I'm quiet but excitable,
Boisterous when set free.
But,
I'm forever on the outside,
Always looking in.

Little Glass Box

I'm living in a little glass box.
Watching everyone live their lives,
Making connections, knowing they're real.
The glass is green with my envy.
Life is passing me by, just out of reach.
I'm shouting! I'm screaming!
No-one hears. My voice just echoes,
Shut in this little glass box.

I'm trapped in a little glass box.
But I need to get out, to be free!
I want a life of my own and to make
connections.
The glass becomes fogged over in black and
grey,
I can't see but I throw myself against the thick
prison walls.
I'm smashing it! The glass is cracking!
My trap shatters, shards showering down,
And I am free from that damn glass box.

I've escaped from my little glass box!
Now I'm surrounded by all those I watched.
They close in on me and there's no connection,
just noise.

Sensations swamp me; drown and overwhelm my senses.

It's too much! I can't cope!

I stumble, glass crunches, I fall, red blood flows. Pain cuts through the pressure in my head.

I understand now that it was never a trap - it was safety!

I am destroyed by the remains of my little glass box.

Vivid Red

The vivid red flows over the white,
The only clear colours in the depths of the night.
Trickling from the innocent scratch upon my
arm,
It doesn't even hurt no more; how can it be
self-harm?
The scars maybe little, but the wounds were so
deep.
There's a problem with them though - they're a
secret I can't keep.
Still, I watch the red flow over the white,
The only clear colours in the depths of the night.

Feeding my Bloodlust

My mind has been twisted,
My existence distorted.
I am a child of the damned,
See the blood upon my hands?
If I grabbed you by the hips,
Your eyes would lock onto my lips,
And then…

Teeth graze skin.
My fangs sink in.
Blood! So sickly sweet,
Down my throat as I feast.
In nothing else I place my trust,
To quell the thirst of my bloodlust.
But it always returns…

Knot Satisfaction

Such satisfaction!
Fancy knot; a Hunters Bend. Reef
Knot alternative.

Galapagos

Grand adventure! A perfect distraction.
Avoiding reminders of grief.
Living in the moment.
Amazing sights and sounds.
Penguins, iguanas, birds, tortoises.
Awe-inspiring views, diverse landscapes.
Great people and beauty all around.
Once in a lifetime?
Sure hope not!

Blue is my Colour

If I had to pick just one shade of blue,
It would be the colour of Sonic the Hedgehog!
But honestly, I like them all.
From the deep dark hues of the sky at night,
And the pale periwinkle shades of flower petals,
To the electric glow of neon lights,
And the comfort of denims and summer skies;
All bring me joy.
The shimmer of royal blues on metals,
That brightens our tech and out transport.
Those greenish blues and hints of grey,
That colour the surface of the sea.
With sky blue topaz and murky agate,
Gold-speckled lapis lazuli,
And almost purple tanzanite,
Nature is full of beautiful blue.
Colbalt, Navy, Peacock,
Ultramarine, Indigo, Azure
Even in paint it has many names,
And I know them,
Because blue is my colour.

The Ray

Mysterious shape
Big, black and menacing. From
The blue emerging.

Tensing, eyes wide. Shark? Danger!
Smooth movements, gliding forward.

Clarity at last!
Big fins pushing through water.
A manta ray swims.

Disbelief as the ray turns,
Looks right at us! Swims away.

Rebel Badge Club

Reconnecting with old passions.
Exploring new interests.
Building a different social circle of,
Enthusiastic, like-minded people -
Lots of laughter ensues.

Branching out, breaking our barriers,
Adventures of all kinds.
Developing skills, dreaming dreams,
Great sense of achievement!
Ever evolving.

Camping for grown-ups.
Loads of supportive people -
Undeniably positive.
Bring on the future!

Haiku

A haiku a day,
Would be an interesting way,
To keep a journal.

To Stain

She was the first, but not the last,
But how I miss her now she has passed.
The little ball of fluff we named Stain,
We loved her lots, but she was a pain.
She was always a small, skinny thing,
Oh, but what joy did she bring.
Hide and seek, under the covers,
So many games; one for each of us lovers.
Cuddles from Mum and food from me,
She even seduced Dad; it was meant to be.
Sometimes she moved like a ninja that Stain the pain.
Another cat like her? That won't happen again.
She will always be my parrot cat, my baby cat,
With her duck feet poses and her flops in my lap.
I really do miss that ball of fluff,
But she had a good life and that is enough.

Slim-ied

Sour and sweet. Slimy, yuck!
I have never understood,
Why my grandad would
Pour single cream over his
Vanilla ice-cream. Bleurgh!

The Escaped Dog?

Out in the autumn chill I walk,
On a mission for chips.
I'm barely off the driveway,
When I hear an unusual sound.
From behind me, to the right comes
A clickity clack...
The tippity tap,
Of claws on the pavement.
Did number 8 get a dog?
Has it escaped?
I turn.
I blink, surprised.
Am I dreaming?
In the middle of the road I stand,
Transfixed.
I stare at the solid beast,
Its' black and white, wiry fur,
Larger in life than imagination...
A badger???
It is a badger!
Just trotting on by me,
As I try to process this sight.
He pauses and looks at me.
Is he as confused by me,
As I am by him?

Then away he goes;
Crossing the road and on,
Up a driveway, to a garden.
I look after him as I go on my own way,
(I still need those chips for dinner)
Did I really just see a badger?
All the way to the shop I ponder.
Was that real? It's so surreal.
All the way I home I still wonder,
Was I dreaming? Did I see it?
I clearly remember the sound,
Of his clickity clack claws.
I really did see a badger,
In the middle of the street!

Penguin-aholic

Pingu started it, I think, my
Ever present love for the
Naughty, cheeky waddlers.
Growing up I was the penguin girl-
Ultimately my defining trait!
I am remembered for loving penguins.
Not faded even after 30 years,
Still happy with penguin themed gifts.

Killer Bacon

Bacon for breakfast,
Perfect! Crispy, delicious...
It tries to kill me.

The tiniest crunchy crumb,
Lodged in my throat, chokes me.

Coughing, eyes streaming,
Don't panic! Dad's... laughing and
Coughing means breathing.

Shifted at last! Finish breakfast.
The next day it happens again.

Bacon for breakfast?
Not if it's crispy, no thanks.
No killer bacon!

Squirrel Brain

One thought in,
One thought out.
I wish it were that simple!
It's more like empty brain,
Slow brain, fuzzy brain,
No focus and then...
BOOM!
10 thoughts at once,
Chasing each other around in my head.
Then one of those thoughts leads to another,
And another,
And yet another!
Until I have no concept at all,
Of getting from thought A,
To thought 83.
And the WHOLE time,
Other thoughts have been escaping.
So that important thing I remembered,
As thought number 35 or 36 (whilst driving)
Is lost by the time I can do something about it.
I know that I'd had a thought,
But I don't know what it was.
If I don't message often,
Blame the squirrel brain!
I probably thought of you at 3am,
And didn't want to risk waking you.

What Jhumbka?

Sway, sway, right stop, left,
Stop. Figure, figure figure.
Right step, left step, eyes.

Eyes, necklace, necklace, earrings.
Wind, wind, stop, stop, shimmy, shim;

Shimmy, shimmy, spin,
Spin, spin, What Jhumbka? ear, down,
Up, up, piano.

Ear, ear, double up, double
Up, piano. Left heart, right,

Heart, bump; bump, bump, bump.
Ear, down, up, up, bend and grab.
What Jhumbka? Spin, bow.

9 789358 314991